IMAGES
of England

WOLVERHAMPTON

*Dedicated to the memory of Frank Mason,
Chief Librarian of Wolverhampton 1952-1976,
who laid the foundation of the collection of photographs
now held at Wolverhampton Archives & Local Studies.
His commitment to local history will leave generations
of future researchers in his debt.*

Proclamation of the death of Edward VII, who died on 6 May 1910. In the days before radio and TV, major events were broadcast by public proclamation. People turned out in very large numbers to hear the news and share in the event. Such proclamations in Wolverhampton took place either in front of the Town Hall in North Street or, as in this case, in Queen Square. Note the schoolgirls in the upstairs window of Coles and the retail market in the background. The shop on the corner of Exchange Street was then W. Hemmings, a china shop.

IMAGES
of England

WOLVERHAMPTON

Compiled by
Mary Mills and Tracey Williams

TEMPUS

First published 1996, reprinted 1999
Copyright © Wolverhampton Borough Council, 1996

Tempus Publishing Limited
The Mill, Brimscombe Port,
Stroud, Gloucestershire, GL5 2QG

ISBN 0 7524 0602 7

Typesetting and origination by
Tempus Publishing Limited
Printed in Great Britain by
Midway Clark Printing, Wiltshire

Front cover illustration
Victoria Street in Edwardian times (see page 45)

Contents

Clearance in progress for the construction of the Penn Road island on the Ring Road in October 1963. Large areas had to be demolished, leading to massive changes in the town's landscape. St Paul's Church can be seen in front of the former Sunbeam factory but it was demolished soon after the photograph was taken. The factory still stands.

Acknowledgements

All of the photographs are from the collection at Wolverhampton Archives & Local Studies, 42-50 Snow Hill, Wolverhampton WV2 4AG. These have come from a variety of sources and, where known, acknowledgements are given below each photograph. Every effort has been made to ensure accuracy and we apologise if anyone has been inadvertently omitted.

The reference numbers given at the end of each caption are those of Wolverhampton Archives & Local Studies.

The authors would like to thank their colleagues and visitors to Wolverhampton Archives & Local Studies who have offered information and encouragement during the compilation of this book.

Introduction

The first written reference to Wolverhampton appears in a charter granted by King Aethelred to the Lady Wulfrun, a Mercian noblewoman, in 985 AD. She was granted land at 'Heantun' (high town) where she endowed the monastery of St Mary in 994. After the Norman conquest the town is referred to as 'Wulvrenehamptonia', and this has developed over the years into Wolverhampton.

The town prospered in the Middle Ages as a result of the wool trade. Raw wool was brought from the Welsh Marches and was spun and woven into cloth. Evidence of this trade can still be seen on the earliest map of the town, surveyed by Isaac Taylor in 1750, which shows several rows of 'tenters', where sheepskins were hung to dry on 'tenterhooks'.

By this time the population of the town had increased to 7,454 as a result of the discovery of coal and ironstone in the district. Industry began to develop, helped by the construction of canals which made it possible to move raw materials and finished products around the country.

Coal mining was established on the eastern side of the town and was mostly on a small scale as much of the coal was near to the surface. Iron working led to the development of a large variety of metal trades for which the town became famous, the area becoming known as the 'workshop of the world'.

The manufacture of locks and keys began in small backyard workshops and was important throughout the region. Production on a larger scale became possible with the introduction of factories such as Chubbs, still a major company in the town. Another important industry was the manufacture of holloware products such as buckets, coal scuttles and kettles. The japanning and enamelling of such products became separate trades. Nineteenth-century trade directories list a myriad of occupations, some of which were highly specialised, such as the manufacture of bucket ears or toasting forks.

During the second half of the nineteenth century the bicycle trade grew in Wolverhampton, with over twenty-five companies involved in the trade by 1892. One of the names listed in the trade directory is that of John Marston, who was originally a tin plate and japanware manufacturer. He later founded the Sunbeam company which became a leading producer of cycles, cars and motor cycles.

Vehicle production and the manufacture of components for the motor industry flourished in the area and, together with Sunbeam, the names of Star, Clyno, Guy, A.J.S. and Villiers, amongst others, made Wolverhampton known all over the world. The 1920s saw the heyday of motor vehicle manufacture in the town, a tradition which virtually ceased with the last production of Norton 'Commando' motorcycles in 1975.

Dependence on the heavy manufacturing and metal-bashing industries brought prosperity to the area in the post-war boom of the 1950s and 60s, resulting in a shortage of workers and an increase in immigration. However, it also made the town vulnerable to the recession that followed and many factories closed down. The modern town is seeking a more diverse economic base although some of the traditional industries still survive.

The 1960s also marked a change in the landscape and boundaries of the town. The slum clearance programmes of the 1950s, followed by the construction of the Ring Road and two shopping centres, dramatically altered the appearance of the town centre. During this process many of Wolverhampton's older properties were lost.

This compilation of photographs encompasses over a century of Wolverhampton's history and aims to give an impression of how life has changed during this period. All of the photographs are from the collection held at Wolverhampton Archives & Local Studies, acquired from many sources over a number of years. Thanks are due to all the people who have taken the time to donate photographs for the benefit of future Wulfrunians. Those taken by Bennett Clark and the Wolverhampton Photographic Society are of particular importance.

The existence of this collection is largely due to the foresight of past librarians from the days of John Elliott, the town's first Chief Librarian, to those of more recent times, including Frank Mason to whom this book is dedicated.

One
Around the Area

Waterloo Road between 1902 and 1928, showing the Baptist Church. At this time the houses were residences for the well-to-do. Many buildings have now now either been demolished or converted into flats or offices. A Lorain tram and Darlington Street Methodist Church can be seen in the background. (C2/WAT/5/2)

Newhampton Road, dating from the early 1920s. The large building in the background was built for the Higher Grade School which opened in 1894. It was occupied by the Municipal Secondary School from 1921 and the Municipal Grammar School from 1945. This school became part of Colton Hills comprehensive school and moved to new premises in 1974. The building subsequently became an annex to Wulfrun College. On the left are fields which are now the site of West Park Schools. In the background is Waterloo Terrace which was built between 1852 and 1855 and is undergoing renovation in 1996. (Brian Perry)

Men haymaking near Newhampton Road in 1904. On the left is Waterloo Terrace, one of the first buildings in Wolverhampton's new town, or New Hampton as the Whitmore Reans area was to be called. On the right are the railings of West Park. (C2/NEWHA/8/5)

Coleman Street, looking towards Newhampton Road West. The Lorain tram dates the picture between 1902 and 1928. The shops on the left are O'Reilly, tobacconist, B.A. Thomas, general store, Whitmore Reans Post Office, B. Bartlem, grocer, and a hardware shop. Across the road, on Newhampton Road, the shops are Charles Jervis, tailor, and an umbrella repair shop. The name 'New Hampton' did not catch on and the area continued to be known as Whitmore Reans. This name may be derived from 'White-moor-reans', a swampy area prone to white fogs or mists and drained by 'reans', gutters running parallel with the furrows of ploughed land. (C1/COL/1/2)

Evans Street, Whitmore Reans. The street is typical of an area built to accommodate the respectable working classes, clerks, etc. Some of the terraced housing still exists but much has been demolished. Corner shops are less in evidence now. As usual, local children are happy to pose for the camera. (C1/EVA/7/1)

Floods in Leicester Street, Whitmore Reans, on 2 July 1914 after over an inch of rain fell in a half-hour downpour at midday. A heatwave had broken on the previous day and, in its report, the *Express & Star* described a severe thunderstorm, intensely vivid lightning and torrential rain, all preceeded by a whirlwind. Elsewhere in the town a man had his hair singed after his hat was struck off his head by lightning. (C1/LEI/6/2)

Hunter Street, Whitmore Reans. There are shops on almost every corner: on the right, the corner of Clifford Street and Newhampton Road, is J. Timmis, Family Grocer; on the opposite corner is Broadheads, a confectioners. The public house facing down Hunter Street is the Five Ways Inn, which stood in Coleman Street where it also joined Hordern Road and Lowe Street. On the left corner of Hunter Street and Newhampton Road is Needhams Chemists advertising drugs and mineral waters. The date is around 1921. (C1/HUN/6/1)

Coleman Street in November 1955. Chester Street leads off to the right. Courtaulds chimney is in the background. The shop on the right is A. Payne. (Wolverhampton Photographic Society no. 97, J. Preece, C1/COL/7/3)

Horseley Fields in 1929. Horseley Field was originally the name of one of the ancient open fields farmed in the Middle Ages but by 1929 it had become a road in the heart of the industrial part of the town. The Horseley Fields railway bridge took the London & North West Railway's Stour Valley line over the road and carried advertising for Butler's Ales, brewed at the Springfield brewery. (C1/HORS/8/1)

Millfields Road, looking towards Wolverhampton, with E. Roberts & Sons, coal merchants, on the right. Workmen are replacing the cobbles with tarmac. (C2/MILL/7/2)

Steelhouse Lane in June 1955, when a photographic survey was made of the town prior to the redevelopment of many areas. The 'Why Not' Inn stood opposite the end of Sutherland Place. It was demolished in the early 1960s along with nearby houses. The present garage on the Bilston Road corner was built on the site. (Wolverhampton Photographic Society no. 71, E.G. Hughes, C2/STEE/5/1)

Dudley Road has been one of the main roads leading from the town centre at least since the time of Isaac Taylor's map of 1750. The people's clothes suggest that this view was taken before 1914. The advertisement for Foster Brothers on the corner of Dudley Road and Bilston Street is little help in dating the photograph as the store has been on the same site since 1906 and nearby since 1899. (C2/DUD/6/1)

Derry Street off the Birmingham Road photographed in June 1955 and showing part of the first council estate built in 1920. To the left of these houses are some much older dwellings which were demolished along with many others during the slum clearance programme after 1955. (Wolverhampton Photographic Society no.114, E.G. Hughes, C1/DER/1/1)

Grove Street in 1955, showing some good examples of old advertisements. (Wolverhampton Photographic Society no. 112, E.G. Hughes, C1/GROV/0/1)

Wolverhampton's first council-built homes were erected on the corner of Cartwright Street and Green Lane, which later became the Birmingham New Road, in 1902 and were demolished in the late 1980s. The design was described as 'Housing of the Labouring Classes, Type no. 5. Cottage Tenement Type'. Waste water closets and washhouses were situated on the landings at the back and shared between four dwellings. The scheme consisted of a block of fifty dwellings and was built at a cost of £5,068. Rent was set at 2s 8d or 3s 8d per week plus 1s 3d rates in order to make the scheme self-supporting. (C2/BIR/3/2-3)

High-rise flats on the Blakenhall Gardens estate, which was opened by Sir Keith Joseph MP on 19 December 1967. Designed by A. Chapman, Borough Architect, the £2,301,997 scheme included 580 flats, 27 houses and 10 shops with flats above. (N5/BLA/2)

Opposite: Another view of the Parkfields area, taken by J. Taylor in 1893, giving a vivid impression of the landscape produced by intensive mine working. Most of the mines in this area were very small scale operations, often no more than gin pits powered by horses. The disused mine buildings appear to have been converted into a home. (A2/PAR/1)

These cottages in Parkfields were photographed in 1941 but would have been built much earlier, when the area was riddled with small coal mines and houses were built randomly with no roadways, planning permission, etc. These were near to Manor Road and the factory behind may be either John Thompson Motor Pressings or the Manor Works. (N4/PAR/E/1)

Villiers Street, showing St Luke's Church. This photograph was taken by Bennett Clark and features people going about their daily affairs. From the clothes it would appear to date from the early 1900s. The terraced houses to the left of the church have all been demolished. (C1/VIL/5/1)

Wolverhampton's first high-rise flats in Dale Street pictured in 1961. The redevelopment of the area to provide 232 dwellings was approved in September 1955 following slum clearance. Most of the new homes were one-bedroom flats and bed-sitting rooms in eight-storey blocks but there were also 27 three-bedroom flats in two-storey terraced blocks and eighty-four two-bedroom flats in three- or four-storey blocks. The flats still stand today. (N5/DAL/1)

The Penn Road around 1910 at the junction with Lea Road. The two trams are of the Lorain surface type, introduced to Wolverhampton in 1902. In the distance can be seen the unmistakable tower of St Peter's Church and the chimney stack belonging to a nearby factory, probably Manders Paint and Varnish works on the site of the modern Mander Centre. On the right are the gates of a large house called Pennhurst. (C2/PEN/6/9)

Drayton Street photographed by Bennett Clark at 4.10p.m. on 15 March 1938. The shop on the left with coats for sale is A.&H.C. Fisher, tailors, clothiers and pawnbrokers. On the corner with Bell Place stands Saunders Valve Co. Ltd. Note the cobbled gutters and the Staffordshire blue brick pavements which used to be common in the Midlands. (C1/DRA/7/1)

An undated Bennett Clark photograph showing the only remaining part of Merridale Farm in Merridale Lane. Merridale Hall stood on this site until it was demolished in 1930. The timber-framed barn which stood nearby was converted into a garage and petrol station and demolished in 1961. The building in this photograph was occupied by a dairy and a paint shop in the early 1960s. (L8/MER/E/2)

Merridale Road in the early part of the century. The Staffordshire blue brick pavements are noticeable on the left. (C2/MERR/7/4)

A turn of the century photograph showing Crawford Street, which later became Crawford Road. The church is Trinity Methodist which stood on the corner of Compton Road. It was designed by George Bidlake and opened in 1863. The land and £1,000 was donated by John Hartley, head of the firm of G.B. Thoneycroft. It was demolished in 1975 and only a war memorial now stands to mark the site. (C1/CRAW/6/1)

Trinity Methodist Church from the Compton Road in the early 1900s. On the right is the old Quarterhouse inn which was replaced by the present public house of the same name in 1934. (C2/COM/8/4)

This picture of Finchfield Hill is believed to date from around 1874, the year when Alexander Staveley Hill was elected as MP for the western division of Staffordshire. The election posters read 'Vote for Staveley Hill, a Staffordshire man'. (C1/FIN/0/1)

A general view of Finchfield, with Broad Lane on the right, Finchfield Road on the left, and what is now Bantock Park stretching into the distance. The widow of Alderman Albert Baldwin Bantock gave the forty-three acres of land and the house known as Merridale House to the Council after her husband's death in 1938. The house, now known as Bantock House, opened as a museum in 1948 following its requisition by the military during the Second World War. (A2/FIN/2)

The Bhylls, Finchfield, built around 1870 for John Clarkson Major (1826-1895) who was in business as a tar distiller. His plant, where he developed pioneering new technology, was between the Birmingham Canal and what is now Major Street, Monmore Green. The house, which was later renamed Bellencroft, was demolished around 1950. (E. Landells, N3/BHY/E/1)

'Shiny' White Oak Drive, off Finchfield Hill, was chosen as the location for a TV washing powder advertisement of the 1960s. The photograph was taken in 1975 since when little has changed. (C1/WHI/5/1)

A view of the Tettenhall Road around 1910. St Jude's church on the left was opened in 1869 with funds given by Miss Mary Stokes and is still standing today. In the distance is the Halfway House public house, so called because it is situated halfway between London and Holyhead. (C2/TET/8/6)

Much has changed since September 1955 when this photograph of Middle Vauxhall, off the Tettenhall Road, was taken. There are two pubs, the Vine on the left and the Rose & Crown on the right. This area underwent slum clearance in 1957-8. (Wolverhampton Photographic Society no. 127, J. Dowdall, C1/MID/5/1)

Two
Town Centre Streets and Housing

Queen Square in 1902, when the public conveniences were built to cater for people visiting the town to attend the Art and Industrial Exhibition. The tram is heading for the exhibition. Photographic evidence shows that hansom cabs waited for customers in this part of the town from at least 1860 and the round building was a shelter for the cabmen. Note the time ball on the roof of the building that is now the Midland Bank. (C3/QUE/8/8)

Wolverhampton town centre in May 1949, with St Peter's Church prominent. The buildings in the foreground are St Peter's School backed by the Technical College, which now fills this whole site as Wolverhampton University. The roof of the wholesale market and the open air market can be seen in the right foreground. In the centre of the picture is the spire of Queen

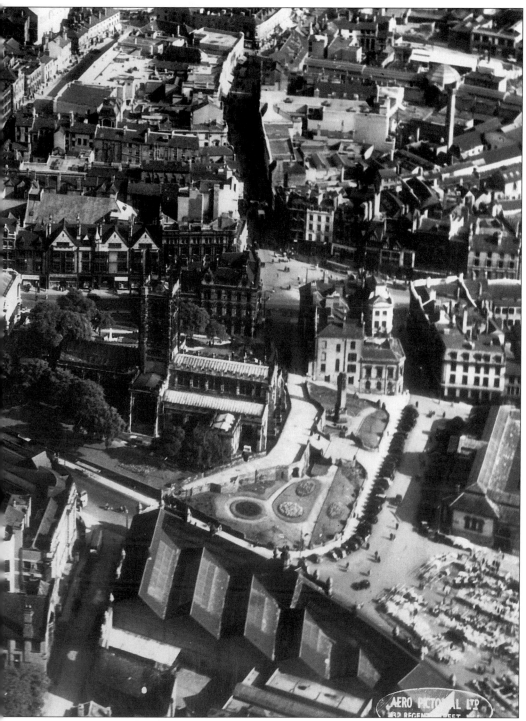

Street Congregational Church and, just above, is St George's Church surrounded by trees. This gives a good impression of the town before the massive changes of the 1960s and the construction of the Ring Road and the Mander and Wulfrun Centres. (Aero Pictorial, A4/5/8)

Chapel Ash, *c.* 1904, at the junction of Merridale Road, Compton Road and Tettenhall Road. In the centre of the photograph is a horse trough and the round building behind it is another shelter for the hansom cab drivers. In front of that is a urinal. The buildings at the junction of Merridale Road and Compton Road were the premises of the Crown Cycle Company. (C1/CHA/7/10)

Another view of Chapel Ash, *c.* 1908. The buildings in the centre are still standing and are now a solicitors. On the right, bearing the name Godsell, is a chemist shop built for Boots Chemists. The plans of this building are in Wolverhampton Archives & Local Studies and are dated December 1908. This building is also still in existence and is undergoing renovation at the time of writing. (C1/CHA/7/14)

Chapel Ash, looking towards the town centre. The spire of St Mark's Church can be seen on the right. P.J. Barnett & Associates won an environmental award in 1994 for the restoration of Waterloo House on the extreme left. Next to it is the Combermere Arms, which was converted from a house to a pub in 1897 and has recently changed its name to Kearney's. An interesting feature of the pub is the lime tree growing in the gents' toilets! (C1/CHAR/8/1)

An almost unrecognisable view of Chapel Ash. When this photograph was taken in 1966 the Ring Road had yet to be built and Darlington Street on the right joined with Salop Street on the left. St Mark's Church still stands but has been converted into offices. (C1/CHA/7/20)

A much older, more unusual photograph of Darlington Street, possibly taken from the roof of the Methodist Church. Much of the area in the foreground is now taken up by the Ring Road island. Opposite St Mark's Church, in Chapel Ash, can be seen the Park Brewery of Wolverhampton & Dudley Breweries. The horse-drawn tram would probably have climbed this steep road rather slowly. Electric trams ran on this line from 1902. (C1/DAR/7/1)

A late nineteenth-century view of Darlington Street from St Mark's Church, showing St Mark's School on the right. The road was cut through in 1821 and named after Lord Darlington, who sold the land to the Town Commissoners. (C1/DAR/8/1)

Darlington Street in the 1950s, looking down to St Mark's Church. On the left is Burtons, which closed in 1992 and now forms part of Beatties' department store. (Brian Perry)

Queen Square, showing the Russian cannon which was captured during the Crimean War and stood on the site from 1858. The cannon was moved to Snow Hill in order to make way for Prince Albert's statue in 1866. According to Alderman W.H. Jones, who wrote a book called *The Municipal Life of Wolverhampton*, published in 1903, it remained there for ten years until people became tired of seeing it and it was returned to the government to be replaced by a gas lamp! (C3/QUE/1/17)

Queen Square between 1876, when the present Barclays Bank was built, and 1902, when the public conveniences were built next to the statue of Prince Albert, consort to Queen Victoria. All the buildings in this photograph still stand, although the statue has been moved several times, most recently in 1991. (C3/QUE/1/19)

34

Queen Victoria surprising everyone by borrowing a sword and knighting the Mayor, John Morris, on 30 November 1866 during the ceremony to inaugurate the statue of Prince Albert. This was the Queen's first appearance in public since Prince Albert's death in 1861 and a story is told that she accepted the invitation after being touched by a letter of sympathy sent by the widows of Wolverhampton at the time of her husband's death. With only nine days notice of the visit, the abundance of decorations throughout the town was amazing. (V1/VIC/2)

Queen Square, looking towards Darlington Street, in 1965. The public conveniences, believed to be the first in the country to cater for women as well as men, were still in use at this time but the statue of Prince Albert has been moved down the road to make way for a traffic island. This area is now pedestrianised and underwent extensive refurbishment in 1991-2 . (C3/QUE/7/33)

Lichfield Street, *c.* 1870, photographed by G.B. Mitchell. This area was mostly demolished following the 1875 Artisans Dwelling Act, which enabled the compulsory purchase of buildings by the local council with the aim of removing sub-standard housing. Lichfield Street became a showpiece shopping and business area, designed to rival Birmingham's Corporation Street. No replacement housing was provided. (C1/LIC/2/1)

The changed aspect of Lichfield Street can be seen in this early twentieth-century picture. The buildings on the right still stand although the shop-fronts are much altered. On the left is the Art Gallery & Museum, built with funds given by Philip Horsman, which was opened in 1884. It was designed by Julius Chatwin of Birmingham and is of Italianate design. (C1/LIC/8/10)

Princes Square in around 1910. All the impressive Victorian buildings still stand, although those adjacent to the Art Gallery were replaced by a building occupied by Midland Bank until 1996. The covered entrance to the building on the left has also disappeared. Most of the shops have now gone, although Parry's ironmongers only closed in 1989. (C3/PRI/7/1)

Lichfield Street, looking towards Princes Square, *c.* 1910, a scene which is easily recognisable today. The Victoria Hotel still stands, as does the Sir Tatton Sykes pub (now Lichfields), which was named after a racehorse. The adjacent building is the showroom of Forder & Co., coach builders, listed in the 1900 Kelly's Directory as 'sole builders of Forder Royal' hansom; by special appointment to HM The Queen'. Next to this is the Wolverhampton District Co-operative store, which closed in 1987 and has recently been converted to a café bar. (C1/LIC/7/10)

Cheapside in around 1870, with the retail market, the Exchange building, and the tower of St Peter's Church on the left. At the top of St Peter's steps is the Saxon pillar, the oldest man-made object in the town. It is obviously a busy thoroughfare and people appear to be buying from the carts. (C1/CHE/8/1)

Wulfruna Street in the early 1930s, when the Wolverhampton and South Staffordshire Technical College (now Wolverhampton University) was under construction. The crowds of men may be returning from a match at the Molineux or finishing a shift at a nearby firm such as Chubb's. The pub is the Olde Lamb Inn advertising 'pure home-brewed ales brewed on the premises'. (C1/WUL/8/2)

North Street in the 1920s-30s. The building on the right of the old Town Hall, converted to shops by this time, was originally the house where the Prebend of Monmore lived. Next to this can be seen the Mitre Temperance Hotel, Jessop's Hotel, Cartlidge Bros, mangle dealers, Grosvenor's fruit shop, and Lawley's shoe shop. On the right is the entrance to the Education Offices and School Clinic, still remembered with horror by former schoolchildren as the location of the school dentist. (C1/NOR/4/10)

North Street, looking towards the Town Hall, which was built in 1869-71 and is now used as magistrates' courts . The old Prebend House stands where the Civic Hall is today and the wall of the Retail Market is on the right. Note the ornate ironwork and lights on the building on the left which is now the Town Hall Tavern. (F1/WOL/A/E/7)

Market Street in the 1930s, looking towards Princes Square. The buildings in the background are the Talbot Hotel and, with the unusual gable, Clarks Stores. Queen Street Congregational Church is on the right. This was built in 1865 and demolished in 1971. (C1/MAR/6/1)

Berry Street, c. 1880. The shop on the corner is a tobacconist; other businesses in the street in 1884 included a fishing tackle dealer, pawnbroker, glazier, hook manufacturer, sawyer, skin dealers and tailors. (C1/BER/8/1)

Pipers Row in the early 1900s, looking from Bilston Street. The advert is for J. Tomkys & Son, wood turner, located at no. 27. (C1/PIP/6/2)

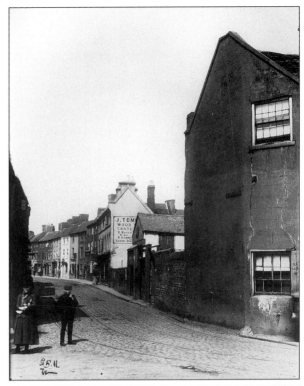

Queen Street around 1890. Until the 1880s Queen Street housed many of the town's most important buildings and was regarded as the main street. Visitors arriving by train passed through the Queen's Building and into Queen Street. However, Lichfield Street became more prestigious after rebuilding so Railway Drive was re-routed to take visitors that way instead . This left the Queen's Building stranded and without a purpose. (C1/QUEE/7/2)

Bilston Street in 1981 at its junction with Market Street, now the site of the Police Station. The Clifton Cinema opened in 1931 on the site of the New Theatre Royal and was demolished in 1981 after having been converted to a bingo hall in 1966. (C1/BIL/1/14)

Church Street in 1955, before redevelopment, with a view up to St John's Church, built in 1755. The public house on the right was the Tiger Inn. (Wolverhampton Photographic Society no.31, A. Darby, C1/CHU/8/1)

Snow Hill in 1902, shortly after the completion of the Central Library. The statue of Charles Pelham Villiers, MP for Wolverhampton 1835-1898, was moved to West Park in 1931. The building behind the statue is the Agricultural Hall, built in 1863 and converted into a cinema in 1913. It was demolished in 1931 and replaced by the Gaumont Cinema. The poster announces a 'Call to Arms' for the 6th South Staffordshire regiment, requiring 550 men, possibly to fight in the Boer War. (C1/SNO/8/2)

Snow Hill in the 1950s, looking from Dudley Street towards the Gaumont Cinema. This was demolished in 1973-4 to be replaced some years later by Allied Carpets. Jays furniture shop is on the right and the building still survives. All the buildings in the foreground, including the Swan and Peacock on the extreme right, were demolished to make way for the Wulfrun Centre. (Brian Perry)

A crowded Victoria Street at its junction with Queen Square in the 1920s. On the right next to Tyler's shoes is Beatties department store, founded on this site in 1877 as the Victoria Drapery Stores. It was rebuilt after a fire in 1896 and was re-fronted around 1929. The fine building on the left is the Queen's Arcade, which was demolished to make way for the Mander shopping centre. A wide variety of vehicles can be seen. (C1/VIC/5/7)

A similar view taken around 1950. Note the art deco elephants on the Burton's building on the right. There are trolleybus wires across the road and a policeman on his bicycle. Parking looks considerably easier than it is today! (C1/VIC/5/12)

Victoria Street, *c.* 1925, showing a
fine array of shoes on display
outside The Carlton Shoe
Company at No. 62, and the
Giffard Arms before it was rebuilt
around 1928. The public house
just visible to the left of the shoe
shop was the Hand & Bottle.
(C1/VIC/4/2)

Victoria Street in Edwardian
times. The half-timbered building
on the right is one of the few to
have lasted to the present day and
is known in the town as Lindy
Lou's. A variety of shops and
businesses can be seen, including
Horace George The Tailor, who
had shops at 18b and 55 Victoria
Street in 1900. Both of his shops
can be seen in this view.
(C1/VIC/6/1)

Worcester Street, looking from Victoria Street, in the 1930s-40s. Blakemore's grocery shop, on the corner of Salop Street, was one of several branches in the town. The buildings in Worcester Street are still much the same although the tenants of the shops have changed considerably. There have also been major changes to the road layout. (C1/WOR/5/2)

Salop Street in the 1950s. Cohen's outfitters on the right still stands although it is now the Red House. The sign underneath the traffic lights reads 'move only on green'. There was an experiment in the town in 1959 to prevent drivers moving off before the light changed to green by omitting red-amber from the sequence. (C1/SAL/7/4)

Great Brickkiln Street, *c.* 1913, a bustling scene with people going about their daily business seemingly oblivious of the camera, except for the interested children in the foreground. On the right is a newsagents and adjacent to it, at No. 15, the entrance to the shop of W. Porter, wood carver. (C1/GRE/0/4)

Bell Street before redevelopment, showing some of the oldest housing in the town. (C1/BEL/2/4)

Court no. 3, Charles Street, in the 1950s. The courts and backyards of streets in Wolverhampton were very overcrowded, containing an estimated 1,639 houses with a population of 6,335. Dwellings in the Charles Street and Herbert Street area, off Stafford Street, were demolished in a slum clearance programme of 1955. At the time, there were 101 houses in the Charles Street Clearance Area, 63 of which had no internal water supply and only one a fixed bath. Only three had an inside toilet and more than half of the houses shared a lavatory. (C1/CHAR/2/4)

Nos 29-38 Charles Street in 1955. Having been compulsorily purchased by the Council, the houses were all vacated by December 1955 and demolished in the following year. In the distance is the Molineux Hotel which was built around 1750 and is now a grade II* listed building. It closed in 1979, since when its condition has deteriorated badly. (Wolverhampton Photographic Society no. 8, J. Dowdall, C1/CHAR/1/2)

Drawing water in a court in Westbury Street in September 1955. At the time of the 1951 census 18 per cent of households in the Wolverhampton borough shared, or were entirely without, a piped water supply. Westbury Street lies off Broad Street and most of the houses have been demolished since this photograph was taken. (Wolverhampton Photographic Society no. 119, George Cadman, C1/WESTB/0/1)

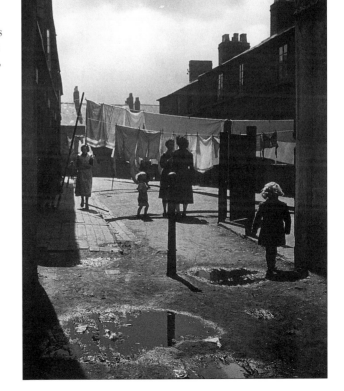

King Edward's Row, which lay between Pearson Street and Pountney Street, in 1952. (Wolverhampton Photographic Society no.24, M.G. Cooper, C1/KING/0/1)

Caribee Island shortly before it was demolished in Wolverhampton's first redevelopment enabled by the Artisans Dwellings Act of 1875. The area was home to a large number of Irish migrants working in collieries, ironworks and in construction trades. Described in 1849 as a 'collection of the most squalid looking houses on the north side of Stafford Street', the area was notorious for crime, grossly overcrowded living conditions and poor sanitation. (C1/CARI/0/1)

A 1913 picture of Townwell Fold, situated between Salop Street, Victoria Street and Darlington Street. The town has several 'folds', the name referring to a time when Wolverhampton's wealth came from the wool trade and sheep were penned in folds. Several 'courts' seem to have been renamed folds and first appear on a map drawn by George Wallis in 1827. Townwell Fold looks rather different today, the only remaining section forming the vehicle access to Beatties department store. (C5/TOW/5/1)

Three
Shopping

Beatties department store, Victoria Street, sometime between 1912, when it was built, and 1929, when the building was re-fronted. Note the window displays on the first floor. (L3/BEA/E/2)

An early 1960s aerial view showing Snow Hill and Dudley Street running across from the junction with Cleveland Street on the left to the top of St John's Street on the right. The town's two old shopping arcades can be seen: the Central Arcade running from Dudley Street to

the bottom of St John's Street, and the roof of the Queen's Arcade on the extreme right in front of Beatties. Changes are obviously already happening, with C&As and Woolworths already constructed and the sites for the Mander and Wulfrun Centres being cleared. (A4/7/3)

The Central Arcade in 1966 shortly before the development of the Mander Centre. In May 1974, while its future was under discussion, it was gutted by a fire which could be seen seven miles away, and had to be demolished. There is still a Central Arcade in the Mander Centre, on approximately the same site, although it lacks the character of the original Victorian structure. (David John Stanley, L2/CEN/I/1)

An unusual picture of Dudley Street in the early 1870s with E.J. Jones, grocers, in the centre and F. Neale, hatters, which stood on the corner of King Street, on the left. (C1/DUD/4/2)

W.B. Cooley's pharmacy shop in Dudley Street, c. 1900. The stock was obviously not limited to medication for people, as a sign in the window proclaims the sale of genuine horse and cattle medicine. The shop, which was four doors away from Neale's in the block between King and Queen Streets, continued in Dudley Street until 1917. (L3/COO/E/1)

Dudley Street, *c.* 1930. Marks & Spencer has signs advertising 'back to school clothes' in its boys wear department as well as ladies' and children's new spring drapery. George Mason's grocery shop was one of many food shops in the town centre, something which has more or less disappeared today. The car parked outside Freeman Hardy Willis, a business already established in Dudley Street in 1884, is a Singer, registered in Wolverhampton in 1929. (C1/DUD/3/5)

Another Bennett Clark photograph showing Dolcis Shoe Shop, Dudley Street. There has obviously been a change in the way shoes are displayed in shop windows! (L3/DOL/E/1)

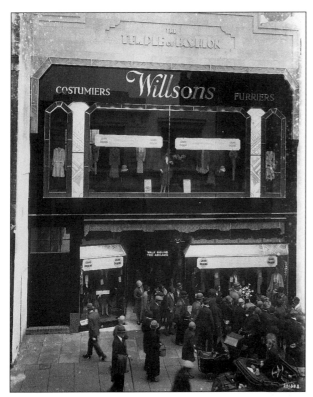

Willsons 'Temple of Fashion', Dudley Street, at its grand opening in the 1920s. The shop was re-fronted in 1937 and the site is now occupied by Marks & Spencer. (L3/WIL/E/1)

Buxton & Bonnett, Dudley Street, photographed by Bennett Clark. The shop closed in September 1979 and moved to 51 Victoria Street. (L3/BUX/E/2)

Dudley Street pictured around the 1920s. On the right is H. Samuel, jewellers, which still exists on the same site, and on the left can be seen Buxton & Bonnett. (C1/DUD/6/17)

Dudley Street, looking towards St Peter's Church, in 1955. Since this date the Central Arcade on the left has been demolished and, in 1973, the forty-nine parking meters in the street were removed and the area pedestrianised. Fosters have been on the same corner since 1906. (C1/DUD/6/12)

Queen Square and the entrance to the Queens Arcade, c. 1910. The lease of the Queens Arcade was taken over by Mander (Holdings) Ltd in 1962 and the arcade was subsequently demolished for the development of the Mander Centre. Unfortunately there are no views of the interior in the Archives & Local Studies collection. (C3/QUE/2/7)

Lipton's grocery stores on the corner of Exchange Street and Queen Square in the 1920s. This is now Consorts Wine Bar. (L3/LIP/E/1)

F.W. Bradford's in Darlington Street, founded *c.* 1890. The firm was taken over by neighbouring Beatties in 1960 following the death of the owner, Frederick J. Bradford, in the previous year. (Brian Perry)

A Bennett Clark photograph of Bennett Clark's shop, 74 Darlington Street. Arthur Bennett Clark was the son of a Bristol photographer who set up his first studio in Wolverhampton in 1887. After his death in 1937 the business was carried on under the Bennett Clark name by his assistants, William Hart and Miss V.M. Parker, until their retirement in 1962. The *Illustrated Towns of England Business Review* dated 1897 describes him thus, 'As an out-door photographer Mr Clark has established a high reputation, his work in landscapes, groups, architecture, etc, being absolutely unsurpassed for artistic merit and first-class finish. His views of Wolverhampton command a large sale.' (L3/BEN/E/1)

One of the most recognisable buildings in Wolverhampton, 19 Victoria Street, is better known as 'Lindy Lou', the name of a children's clothes and equipment shop which occupied the premises in the 1960s and 70s. Probably built at the end of the sixteenth century, it is recorded as the Hand Inn in 1609. It was used as a bakery in the nineteenth century and, after restoration in 1981, it housed the Welfare and Consumer Advice Centres until recently. (L3/LIN/E/5)

W.H. Smith & Son, Lichfield Street, in the 1920s. Circulating libraries, where people paid a subscription to borrow books, were popular but gradually died out as the concept of free public libraries spread. Originally public libraries were seen as a means of self-education for the working classes whilst those who could afford it joined subscription libraries. As attitudes changed and financial pressures on the middle-classes increased, public libraries became seen as libraries for all and the use of subscription libraries declined, particulary during the depression years of the 1930s. (L3/SMI/E/1)

Staff outside the shop of Edwin Bates, Worcester Street c. 1912. (Ned Williams, L3/BAT/E/1)

Edwin Blakemore's grocery shop, Chapel Ash, which closed in October 1971 after about forty years on the site. (L3/BLA/E/1)

The Home & Colonial Stores started in 1885 and had a number of shops in the town, this one being at 176 Newhampton Road East. The photograph was taken in the early 1920s, just before the opening of the branch. (L3/HOM/E/11)

Mac Fisheries, 62 Chapel Ash. This picture is believed to date from the 1930s and the sign above the entrance reads 'Pelham Anderson licensed to deal in game'. On the left, at No. 64, is Hinde's tobacconists, and on the right can just be seen the Little Gallery for antiques, unique glass, china, hand-made pottery, decorative craft work and gifts. (L3/MAC/E/1)

A wonderful display for a window dressing competition for the magazine *Tobacco*. The shop is believed to be at 57 Snow Hill but the date is difficult to establish. The style of dress of the people reflected in the advertising signs on the right suggests the period before the First World War. (L3/TOB/E/1)

The Retail Market, Cheapside, in the early twentieth century. Opened in 1853, the building lasted for over a hundred years until the market moved to a new site in 1960. The elegant iron pillars were both decorative and practical. They were hollow and carried rainwater from the roof into the drains. In 1871 policemen were employed on a temporary basis to rid the place of 'unruly boys and others who attended the hall for no other purpose than loitering'. (L1/RET/I/1)

The new Retail Market on the corner of School Street and Salop Street, photographed from the Dale Street flats in 1961. Built at a cost of £508,000, it was officially opened on 22 June 1960. St Peter's Church can be clearly seen on the skyline, as can the floodlights of the Molineux ground on the left. Work began in May 1996 on a new outdoor market in School Street. (L1/RETA/E/3)

An early twentieth-century view of the Market Place in St Peter's Square, showing the Market Hall on the right. The right to hold markets in Wolverhampton dates back to a royal charter of 1258 which allowed markets to be held weekly on a Wednesday. However, there were markets in the town earlier than this as, in 1180, the inhabitants of the town were ordered to pay a fine for holding a market without a licence. (L1/STP/E/6)

The Market viewed from St Peter's Gardens in 1954. On the right is Giffard House, built between 1727 and 1733 as a Mass House and priest's residence. A chapel was incorporated into the house so that Catholics could attend Prayers or Mass which, at that time, were illegal. In 1826 a separate chapel was built adjoining the house. Renovated in 1989-90, Giffard House is a Grade II* listed building. (Wolverhampton Photographic Society no. 29, A. Darby, L1/STP/E/17)

This appears to be a delivery of Cherry Blossom Boot Polish being made to Craddock's in Queen Square in the 1930s. Stephen Craddock, born in Northampton in 1853, was a prominent figure in Wolverhampton until his death in 1925. (C3/QUE/2/11)

George Dugmore's cycle shop at 253-257 Bilston Road, April 1912. In the shop doorway are Dorothy Dugmore and her parents, Susan and George Dugmore, with Ethel Dugmore holding a Rudge Whitworth child's cycle. On the right is Harry Evans, errand boy, about to take a wheel to the plater. (Ned Williams, L3/DUG/E/1)

Four

Work

Gin pits at Parkfields. This photograph illustrates the way coal was often extracted in this part of the Midlands. The pit was little more than a basic bell pit where a short shaft was sunk and the coal was extracted around the base until it became unsafe to remove any more. Then the horse-powered gin, used to lower the men and tools and raise the coal, was simply dismantled and moved to where a new shaft could be sunk and the whole process repeated. These small pits were not properly mapped, which accounts for the numbers of shafts which unexpectedly appear in the area from time to time. (L6/GIN/2)

Chubb's Lock & Safe Co., Chubb Street. This five-storey building was built in 1899 and, following refurbishment in 1990-1, now houses the Lighthouse Media Centre and Cinema. The firm of Chubb's is now in premises on the Wednesfield Road. (L6/CHU/E/1)

Lock making at Chubb's in 1911. The first Chubb lock was invented in Portsmouth in 1818, although the firm did not open a factory in Wolverhampton until 1841 when it moved into the premises of the old workhouse in Horseley Fields. Chubb's was taken over by Racal in 1986 but became independent again in 1992. (L6/CHU/I/1)

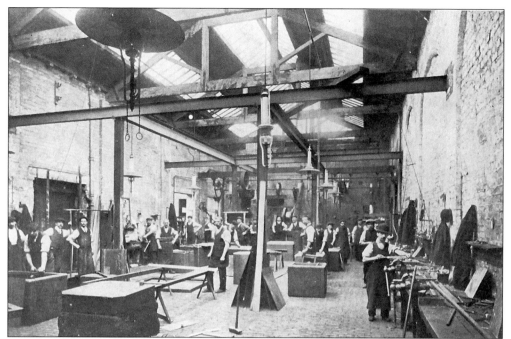

George Price, safemakers, Church Lane, in 1911. The company introduced a furnace on the premises to case-harden safe doors to make them drill-proof. In addition to safes, the firm also produced unpickable and gunpowder-proof locks. (L6/PRI/I/1)

The Shakespeare Foundry of T.&C. Clark & Co. Ltd, Horseley Fields, 1911. The company made enamelled cast-iron pots, pans, kettles, etc. and was established in 1795. It was taken over in 1962 by an American firm, A.O. Smith, by which time it was producing enamelled chemical plant and glass-lined steel equipment for breweries and the chemical industry. (L6/CLAR/I/1)

One of Wolverhampton's most famous firms, the Sunbeam Motor Car Co., Upper Villiers Street, Blakenhall. The company was founded by John Marston for the manufacture of pedal cycles, although its first horseless carriage was running in 1899. The Sunbeam motor cycle was introduced in 1912 and the firm was also involved in the early production of aeroplane engines. In the foreground is St Luke's Church and Marston Road leads off towards the right. (L6/SUN/E/1)

Opposite: The Sunbeam Silver Bullet on a test rig. The car was over thirty feet long and was built to make an attempt on the world land speed record of 231.44 m.p.h. It was shipped to Daytona, America in 1930 to be driven by Kaye Don, but the attempt was unsuccessful, unlike a previous attempt in 1927 when Sir Henry Segrave, driving Sunbeam's 1000 h.p. Scarlet Monster, became the first to exceed 200 m.p.h. (Chris Minors, L6/SUN/I/5)

Workers leaving Sunbeam's Cycle and Motor Cycle works, 'Sunbeamland', in Paul Street. The building still stands by the Penn Road island and is now C.E. Marshall's. (L6/SUN/E/3)

Viking Cycles, Merridale Works, Russell Street *c.* 1959. Established in 1908 in Heath Town, the firm moved to Wolverhampton in 1928. The name was very well known and cycles were exported to almost every country in the world. The production of Viking Cycles ceased in 1967 although the company continued to supply cycles built by other manufacturers. (L6/VIK/I/1)

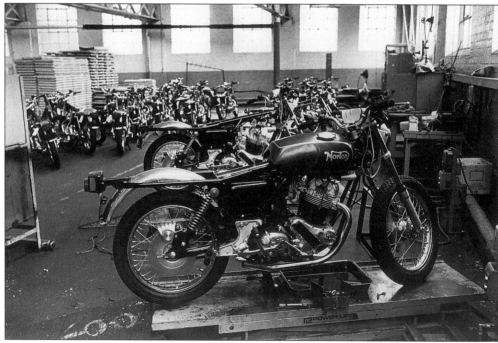

Norton Commando motor cycles at Norton Villiers Triumph, Marston Road. The business went into liquidation in August 1975, although the 1,500 motor cycles remaining in the factory were completed in 1977 by a co-operative of former workers. (Nick Hedges, L6/NOR/I/3)

Road-testing AJS motor cycles at Graiseley Hill in 1927. The leading rider is Bill Huxtable on a 498cc Model H9 De Luxe Touring side-valve single with mechanical oiling. In the row behind him are, left to right: Jim Haddock, Jack Price, and Clarrie Wise looking down at his 349cc Sports. On the extreme left is Frank Turley and, wearing a flat cap in the middle of the three, at the back is Hubert Millard. The firm was founded in the 1890s by the Stevens Brothers. (Ken Millard, L6/AJS/E/3)

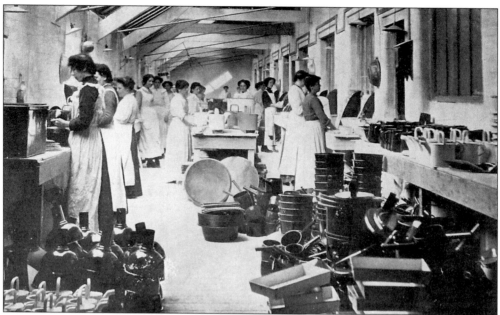

Enamelling at Orme, Evans & Co., Great Brickkiln Street, *c.* 1911. The firm was established in 1864 as Orme Brothers and produced enamelled holloware, including buckets and enamelled advertising plates. (L6/ORM/I/1)

H.M. Hobson's Accuracy Works in Cousins Street. Women workers are much in evidence in this photograph which was taken during the First World War. Established on the site in 1911 to produce Claudel carburetters, the firm became famous for manufacturing components for the aviation industry. In 1919 the R.34 airship, using Claudel-Hobson carburetters, became the first dirigible to cross the Atlantic in both directions. The firm was aquired by Lucas Industries in 1970 and became part of Lucas Aerospace Limited. (L6/HOB/I/1)

The assembly of Villiers cycle freewheels which were then sent on a conveyor belt to the inspection and packing bays, c. 1959. (L6/VIL/I/2)

One of the finishing departments at Wolverhampton Steam Laundry, Sweetman Street, Whitmore Reans, c. 1911. (L6/WOLV/I/2)

Horse-drawn vehicles in St James's Square, *c.* 1900. (C3/STJA/0/1)

A busy scene in Dudley Road near to the junction with Drayton Street, probably in the early 1920s. The workmen are repairing one of the tram lines from the Lorain tram system . Trams were supplied with electricity by boxes set into the road. The system was troublesome and at times dangerous, and was later replaced by overhead wires. The tram in the photo has Snow Hill 1 on the front. (C2/DUD/6/6)

Chapel Ash, *c.* 1910, showing John E. Knight florists shop and advertising for S.&C. Clark's motor works, the entrance to which was in Bath Road. (C1/CHA/8/5)

The Midland Counties Dairy on the corner of Lea Road and Penn Road on 7 September 1966. In the 1960s it was regarded as a model production plant and the staff included 1,000 roundsmen serving 300,000 homes. The dairy closed in 1984 and was demolished in 1988. It is now the site of McDonalds drive-in restaurant. (L8/MID/E/3)

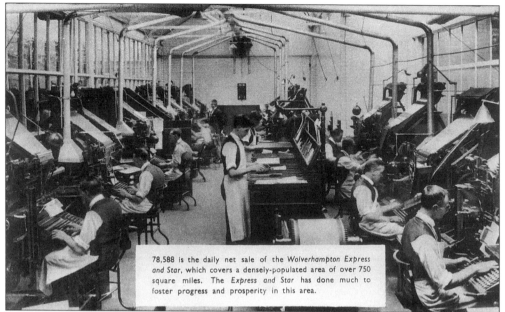

78,588 is the daily net sale of the *Wolverhampton Express and Star*, which covers a densely-populated area of over 750 square miles. The *Express and Star* has done much to foster progress and prosperity in this area.

The *Wolverhampton Express & Star* offices, Queen Street *c.* 1935. The town's first daily evening newspaper, the *Midland Counties Evening Express*, was first published on 2 November 1874. Six years later a rival publication, the *Evening Star*, was produced and after four years of competition, the two newspapers were amalgamated in 1884 as the *Express & Star*, under the ownership of the Midland News Association, chaired by Thomas Graham. (L7/EXP/I/2)

The works of John Steen & Co., printers, in St John Street, 1896. This building was the old Grammar School, founded *c.* 1512, until 1875, when the school moved to its current premises on Compton Road. (L6/STE/E/1)

Five

Leisure

Easter Fair on Brickkiln Patch, 1955. This site had been cleared of sub-standard housing in the 1930s and was later used for the new retail market. On the left can be seen the spire of St Mark's Church. (Wolverhampton Photographic Society, no. 37, M.G. Cooper, V4/BRI/2)

The Central Library's children's section in June 1922. The children's library is still in the same location today, although rather changed in appearance! (Z3/CHI/3)

The official opening of the Central Library on 11 February 1902. In the first archway, between the policeman and the Mayor's Sergeant, are Charles Paulton Plant (Mayor), Aldermen S. Craddock and Joseph Jones. The library was built to commemorate the Diamond Jubilee of Queen Victoria in 1897 and a competition was held to find the best design. A plan by Henry T. Hare was chosen although the resulting building is slightly different from his original design. The foundation stone was laid in 1900 by the Duke of York who later became George V. (Z3/1)

The Wolverhampton Art & Industrial Exhibition, 1902. Held in West Park, the exhibition opened in May for six months and boasted such attractions as a miniature railway and the 'House of Many Troubles', an intricate maze. Many Wolverhampton firms had stands, including Chubbs and the Star Cycle Co. On the left is the Canada Hall, which housed exhibits from Canada, including 10,000 samples of 500 different types of grain. (V3/1902/E/22)

During the exhibition there were Swan boat rides on the lake, which proved very popular, as did the Canadian water chute. Boats were hauled up an inclined plane then released down the chute and across the lake. However, the boat carrying Colonel Thomas Thorneycroft of Tettenhall Towers hit the water askew and the Colonel was thrown against the side of the boat. He never recovered properly and died on 6 February 1903. (V3/1902/44)

The Grand Theatre, Lichfield Street, opened on 10 December 1894 with a performance by the D'Oyly Carte Opera Company of Gilbert & Sullivan's 'Utopia Ltd'. Financial problems caused the theatre's closure in 1980 but it re-opened in 1983 after fund-raising efforts by the Save the Grand Theatre Action Group and a subsidy from Wolverhampton Borough Council. (M8/GRA/E/2)

A performance of the *Desert Song* by Wolverhampton Opera Company at the Grand Theatre in 1935. (Taylor's Press Service, Birmingham, Y8/OPE/6)

The Empire Palace of Varieties, Queen Square, c. 1910. The theatre was built in 1898 and became the Hippodrome in 1921. Performers included Peter Sellers, Phyllis Dixey and Joe Loss and his band. Fire destroyed most of the building in 1956 and it was eventually sold to developers who demolished the rest. The new development was occupied first by Times Furnishings and more recently by Poundstretcher. Yates's Wine Lodge opened on the site in June 1996. (M8/EMP/E/9)

Tempest Street on 18 November 1963, showing the overnight queue for concert tickets to see the Beatles who were appearing at the Gaumont on the following day. The *Express & Star* of 20 November 1963 described scenes of mass hysteria, with one girl feigning suicide in an attempt to see the group. Reporters commented that it was impossible to hear the band because of the screams of the audience. (Graeme Crowe, C1/TEMPE/5/2)

The Strand picture house, Coleman Street, c. 1914. The gentleman in the top hat may be H.J. van Lachterop, manager. The lady on the right was Mrs Emma Egginton (née Cartwright), and the lady on the left with the hat, Miss Nell Egginton. (Information from Mrs Robinson, M7/STR/E/1)

The Gaumont Palace Cinema on the corner of Snow Hill and St George's Parade in 1934. The site is now occupied by Wilkinson's. (Herbert Felton, M7/GAU/E/6)

The Queens Cinema, Queen Square. This was Wolverhampton's eighth cinema and it opened in September 1914. A tea room in the building added to the upmarket atmosphere. The cinema was converted into a dance hall and opened as the Queens Ballroom in 1959. It was demolished in 1977-8 and the site was redeveloped by Lloyds Bank in 1980. (M7/QUE/I/2)

The ABC Cinema on the corner of Bilston Street and Garrick Street in 1981. Built in 1938, the building was the Savoy Cinema until 1960. It later became the Canon Cinema and closed in November 1991, the last film shown being *Out for Justice*. The building is currently being converted into a leisure complex. (M7/ABC/E/1)

A granite boulder in West Park weighing six tons, thought to have come from Grifell Mt, Kircudbrightshire, during the glacial period. It was found in Wolverhampton cemetery in 1880. The park was designed by R.H. Vertegans, one of twenty-seven competitors who entered a design. It opened on 6 June 1881 on the site of the town race course, which moved to Dunstall. (M1/WES/48)

West Park conservatory was opened in 1896 at a cost of £1,500, which was met by the proceeds of the 1893 Floral Fete. This Grade II listed building is the only surviving example of a Victorian park conservatory in the Black Country and was re-opened in 1996 following restoration. (M1/WES/60)

Ice skating on the frozen lake in West Park. The lakes were formed by combining the water from the swampy land with water from the well in the grounds of the public baths. When the lake froze, as it did several times, ice skating was allowed. (M1/WES/5)

A Bennett Clark photo of the boating lake at East Park, *c.* 1900. The park was opened in 1895 and was described as an 'excellent resort for the toiling thousands' of residents from the eastern side of Wolverhampton. There were problems with water seeping out of the lake into the old mineworkings below and, as a Festival of Britain project in 1951, the empty lake was redeveloped as a children's playground. (M1/EAS/1)

The 1939 Wolverhampton Wanderers FA Cup final squad before the kick-off of the match with Portsmouth. Tommy Galley is shaking hands with King George VI and Wolves captain Stan Cullis is making the introductions. Portsmouth won 4-1. (Y8/WOL/4)

Members of the Wolverhampton Tricycle Club in the late nineteenth century. Note the Penny Farthing on the right. (J.S. Roper, Y8/TRI/1)

The Central Swimming Baths, Bath Avenue, c. 1900. The 134-year-old building was demolished in 1985 after engineers found it to be structurally unsound. The present swimming baths opened on the site in 1990. (M1/CEN/l/5)

James's Turkish baths in Albany Road, off Darlington Street, in the early 1900s. An advertisement in the Wolverhampton Red Book of 1901 indicates that it was open daily for both ladies and gentlemen from 9a.m. to 10p.m. and that the cure of nerve complaints and lead poisoning was a speciality, with 37 out of 41 cases being cured in 1899! The building was demolished in 1966 during the building of the Ring Road. (C2/ALB/3/1)

The Victoria Hotel, Lichfield Street, in the early twentieth century. The hotel still exists on the same site. Shops on the left include: Bottley's Herb Beer Saloon; a newsagent; Cook & Son's excursion and tourist office issuing tickets for the Midland Railway (operating out of the High Level station) and the Great Western (from the Low Level station). (L4/VIC/E/3)

The interior of the Victoria Hotel dating from around the 1920s according to its appearance. Although the exterior has changed little the interior has been altered considerably. (L4/VIC/I/1)

Reynold's restaurant, 18 Queen Square, in the 1920s. This was a meeting place for people who lived in the town and was considered a suitable place for young men to entertain their lady friends. According to their advertisement in Kelly's Directory, the firm was established in 1723. The restaurant closed in 1966 and the Wolverhampton Tourist Centre now occupies the building. (L4/REY/I/1)

A photograph of the Midland café, 15 Queen Square, taken by G.B. Mitchell sometime before 1908. O.E. McGregor, a baker and confectioner, ran this restaurant from 1884 until 1908 when it was taken over by J. McGregor, possibly his son. The shop on the left belonged to Alfred Baker, a stationer. The Midland café later became Lyons café which closed some time between 1967 and 1970. The building was occupied by the Halifax Building Society after 1970. (L4/MID/E/1)

The Feather's Inn, North Street. The pub was originally the 'Plume Of Feathers' and stood in the block between Tinshop Yard and Lawyers Field when this early photograph was taken. It was re-built on the same site between 1902 and 1919 and still stands today in the re-named Molineux Street. The pub was run by J. Piper from 1884 until 1892 but William Poole does not appear in the trade directories. The advertisements are of interest: there are three different brands of stout on offer, with Imperial stout selling for 2d a pint. The licensee was also able to sell wines, spirits and tobacco. Some licences only permitted the sale of beers. (J. Smallshire, L4/FEA/E/3)

The Molineux Hotel (1950) was originally built as a town house for the Molineux family in around 1750. The house and grounds were bought by O.E. McGregor in 1860 and the grounds became pleasure gardens and sports fields open to the public. He was granted a licence to sell spirits in 1870. Wolverhampton Wanderers Football Club began to meet in the hotel around this time and eventually bought the grounds to become the site of their football stadium, still called The Molineux. The hotel closed in 1979 and the building still stands, between the football ground and the ring road, but it is derelict and despite numerous schemes and remarks by the Prince of Wales still awaits renovation. (L4/MOL/E/6)

The Star and Garter public house in Victoria Street. This building, which was demolished in 1964, is remembered with affection by many local people. It stood opposite Beatties next to the Queens Arcade and was replaced by the Mander Centre. The oldest view of it is taken from a painting dated 1635. This photograph was taken in the nineteenth century after the exterior had been rebuilt. (L4/STA/E/6)

Opposite: The Queen's Hotel on the corner of Cheapside and North Street. The licensee was Cecil G. Godley (or possibly Codley). The small sign hanging on the single storey section on the left says 'Wine Bar' and the larger one 'Bent's Brewery Limited'. The building to the left is the back of the Empire Palace (later the Hippodrome). The building is still a public house and wine bar which was renovated and re-named Brannigans a few years ago. It is now called No Great Shakes. (L4/QUEE/E/4)

The Parkfield Tavern, Parkfield Road, which looks as if it has been converted from a row of houses. The photograph appears to date from the 1930s or 40s. One of the boys is wearing a pair of sturdy boots and the other a pair of very heavy looking football boots. The pub still stands although it looks somewhat smarter now. (L4/PARKF/E/2)

The Halfway House public house, Tettenhall Road, in the early years of the twentieth century. The advert on the side gives the name John Cook and advertises Good Stabling. The delivery van belongs to J.S. Beddow, Wholesalers. (L4/HAL/E/2)

Six

Religion

St John's Church when St John's Square was still intact. The church was built in 1755 by Roger Eyken, who may also have been the designer, and looks much the same today, although it has undergone several restorations. The surrounding square has changed more, with the Ring Road now in the place of the houses on the right, the south side. Only the east side is still intact, modern office blocks on the other two sides lessening the impact of the building. The church houses the famous 'Renatus Harris' organ. Built in 1633, it was on its way from Dublin to London for repair in 1762 and had reached Wolverhampton when the owner died. Representatives of St John's were able to persuade his widow to sell it for £500. (E1/STJO/E/5)

St Peter's Collegiate Church, which lies at the centre of the town on the site of the original minster church dedicated to the Blessed Virgin Mary, rebuilt by Lady Wulfrun. This impressive building dates from 1425 and stands now much as it did in the sixteenth century, with the exception of the chancel which was completely rebuilt in 1867. The lower section of St Peter's Gardens in front of the church were laid out in around 1894 on part of the former graveyard. The Horsman fountain was switched on in 1896 and has recently been restored. There are also plans to refurbish the gardens, the only green space in the town centre, which include replacing the railings melted down during the Second World War. (E1/STPE/2/42)

An unusual view of St Peter's taken before the upper section of St Peter's gardens was laid out on the site of the old graveyard around 1936. In the foreground is the roof of the retail market and the building on the left is the Technical College, now Wolverhampton University. The photograph may have been taken from the top of the old town hall. (Mr Eisenhofer, E1/STPE/4/29)

St George's Church, photographed after services had ceased to be held in 1978. The broken windows and general air of dereliction show that the building could have been lost, but it has been preserved, albeit as part of a Sainsbury's supermarket. The church was designed by James Morgan of London and consecrated in 1832. Cholera victims were buried here in 1849 and the graveyard closed in 1851. In 1898 the churchyard was turned into a park, open to the public. The remains of people still buried in the graveyard were moved in 1981 to make it possible to redevelop the site. (E1/STGE/E/16)

The interior of St George's. This now forms the entrance to the supermarket which opened in 1987. Unfortunately none of the internal features were in a suitable condition to be preserved during the restoration. (E1/STGE/I/2)

St Mark's Church and Schools, Chapel Ash, viewed from Darlington Street and photographed by Bennett Clark. The church was built after Darlington Street was constructed and was consecrated in 1849. Steen and Blacket's Wolverhampton Guide published in 1871 complained that the spire, although impressive, spoiled the view from Queen Square out towards the Clee Hills! The church ceased to be used for worship in 1979 and was converted into offices in 1989. The schools were also opened in 1849 and moved to new premises during the Second World War. The building had been demolished by 1956. (E1/STM/E/7)

The interior of St Mark's decorated with flags to mark an unknown occasion. The 1871 guide commented that the church '... may be more commended for its internal than external architecture'. It also reported that most of the seats were free and a large proportion of the congregation were from the working classes. (E1/STM/I/1)

98

All Saints Church and school. The original school and church were established in a converted pigsty in Steelhouse Lane in 1864 as a mission church of St John's. The present church opened in 1879 and still stands, although most of the building is now a community centre and just one chapel is used for religious worship. The school building immediately next to the church dates from 1895. (E1/ALL/E/1)

Stonelaying at St Chad's Church, Owen Road, on 25 January 1908. The church opened later that year on 28 November. (E1/STCH/E/1)

The interior of St Mary's Church, Stafford Street, which closed in 1948 and was demolished. Some of the stained glass was taken to St Peter's. (E1/STMA/I/2)

St Matthew's Church, Lower Walsall Street. This church was designed by E. Banks and the foundation stone was laid in 1848 by G.B. Thorneycroft, then Mayor of Wolverhampton. The church was consecrated in the following year. It occupied a prominent position on a triangle of land between Causer Street, Horseley Fields and Lower Walsall Street. The photograph was taken in April 1955. The church was demolished in 1964 and replaced by a new building on the Willenhall Road. (Wolverhampton Photographic Society no. 27, B. Shelley, E1/STMAT/E/1)

Christ Church, which stood at the Five Ways junction on the corner of Dunstall Road and Waterloo Road. The photograph dates from the first part of the twentieth century. The church was opened in 1868 and demolished in 1975. Part of the site was used when the junction was altered and the vicarage was converted into a mosque, which still stands. (E1/CHR/E/4)

Snow Hill Congregational Church, which stood where the Whiteheads building is now. The notice on the railings reads 'People's Service every Sunday afternoon from 3 o'clock to ... o'clock in Temple Street Lecture Hall. All over 17 welcome.' These services were generally directed at working class people and women in particular. In 1941 the west gable of the church collapsed and the whole building had to be demolished. Services were held in the memorial hall until 1964, when the congregation moved to the newly opened Congregational Church on the Penn Road. (E3/SNO/E/2)

SS Peter & Paul Church, North Street, viewed from Chapel Yard. The church adjoins Giffard House and was built onto an existing chapel inside the house, opening in 1828. Alterations were made in the 1850s and the Lady Chapel was added in 1930. Plans were made to demolish both house and chapel in the 1980s but they were reprieved after a public outcry and renovated in 1989-90. They now stand in an isolated position close to the Ring Road. (E2/SSPE/E/4)

St Patrick's Roman Catholic Church and schools, Westbury Street. The original school and mass centre opened in Littles Lane in 1849 to cater for the large number of Irish immigrants who settled in this part of town after the potato famines of the 1840s. The church pictured was built in 1869 and closed in 1972 when a new church opened on Wolverhampton Road, Heath Town. The school moved to Bagnall Street in 1914 as a primary and girls' secondary school. In 1970 the primary school moved to Graiseley Lane and the girls' secondary became part of St Edmund's. (John Beswick, E2/STPA/E/2)

An ordination service at SS Mary & John Roman Catholic Church, Snow Hill, which took place on 29 September 1929. It was the first such service held in the church and was led by the Roman Catholic Archbishop of Birmingham, Dr Williams. (Mr Eisenhofer, E2/SSMA/I/4)

The original Darlington Street Wesleyan Methodist Chapel, which opened in 1825 and was capable of seating 1,600 people. It stood on the same site as the present church and there were schools for boys, girls and infants behind the church in School Street, which closed around 1910. (E3/DAR/E/2)

The opening of the new Darlington Street Methodist Chapel on 29 October 1901. This was clearly a major event as a vast crowd has assembled for the ceremony. The new building was in a different style from the older, more austere chapel, with the large dome a distinctive feature. (E3/DAR/A/E/1)

Seven

Education

Wolverhampton and South Staffordshire Technical College, Wulfruna Street, now part of
Wolverhampton University, photographed soon after its opening in 1933. The main entrance
is commonly referred to as the 'marble' today. This building has changed little although there
have been many buildings added over the years and the university now occupies a much larger
site. When it first opened the main aim was to provide the industrial community with '... an
unfailing reservoir of technically-trained men and women'. (I1/POL/E/2)

Wolverhampton Grammar School on the corner of Merridale Lane and Compton Road. This photograph was taken in 1890 shortly after this building opened. Before this time the school, which was founded in 1512, was located in St Johns Lane, off Dudley Street. These buildings are still in use although many extensions and new buildings have been added over the years. (I3/GRM/E/12)

A general view of the Wolverhampton High School for Girls, which was established in 1911 with 180 girls. There was also a mixed Kindergarten but the last boys left in 1923. The school was originally jointly run by Wolverhampton and Staffordshire Councils, taking an equal number of pupils from each area. From 1927 it took a third of its pupils from Staffordshire. The school chose to remain a grammar school when the comprehensive system was introduced into the town and became Grant Maintained in 1990. Judging by the dress of the PE teacher this photograph was taken shortly after the school opened. (Alex Chatwin, I3/GHS/E/14)

A science laboratory at the Girls' High School. Science was introduced as an 'A' level subject in 1918. (13/GHS/I/2)

Pupils from the Girls' High School tending their allotments during the First World War. At that time the school was clearly on the edge of the town with open views over the countryside. (13/GHS/E/7)

A Bennett Clark photograph from the 1890s of St Peter's School, St Peter's Walk. At this time it was an elementary school for boys and girls. In 1901 new schools for boys and girls were built in St Peter's Square and some of these buildings were used as part of the university until their demolition in 1996. The boys' secondary school moved to the Compton Park schools site in 1965 and the girls joined them in 1974. (I3/STPE/E/2)

St Peter's Boys' School football team in 1934, when they had won the Sir Alfred Bird Cup. The three staff are, left to right: W. Clinton, A.E. Jackson, P. Goldby. The boys are, back row: A. Rogers, Walters, Trow, Rowley, A. Whittle, Miller, J. Stokes. Front row: D. Gough, D. Bayliss, J. Colley (Captain), T. Laine, A. Leach. (Anthony Whittle, Y5/STPE/1)

*The Municipal Secondary School
Wolverhampton.*

The Hall.

The Hall of the Municipal Secondary School, Newhampton Road, in 1923. The school was set up in 1921 in buildings that had formerly been used by the Higher Grade School, which had moved to Old Hall Street. In 1944 it became the Municipal Grammar school and during the 1950s was the only co-educational grammar school in the town. In 1974 it amalgamated with Graiseley and Manor Secondary Schools to form Colton Hills Comprehensive School which moved to new purpose-built premises in Goldthorn Park in 1975. (University College, Lampeter, I3/MUN/I/2)

1935.

Pupils from the Municipal Secondary School pose in the Gymnasium in 1935. (University College, Lampeter, I3/MUN/I/6)

Brickkiln Street School, Great Brickkiln Street, one of the oldest schools in the town still in use today. The buildings look much the same from the outside, although the tower is no longer there. The school was one of the original Board schools opened by Wolverhampton School Board, established in response to the 1870 Education Act. It opened in 1878, replacing schools attached to Queen Street and Temple Street Chapels. (I3/BRI/E/1)

A classroom in Brickkiln Street school in around 1928. Miss Olive Perry, who died in 1995

Dudley Road School opened in 1873 and was also one of the original Wolverhampton Board Schools. The photograph appears to date from around the turn of the century. The notice board says that it caters for Boys, Girls and Infants and gives the opening hours. The school closed in 1986 and most of the pupils and staff went to Graiseley Primary School. The building is now used as a community centre. (I3/DUD/E/2)

aged 75, is in the third row from the front, third from the right. (Hazel Woodward, Y5/BRI/2)

All Saints School cricket team in 1960, winners of the Primary Schools' Cricket League. The boys are back row, left to right: Clive Hole, John Disley, Roger Bryan (?), Melvyn Hartland, Kevin Long(?), Michael Hartland, Derek Lawrance. Middle row: Laurie Light, Richard Gullock, David Morgan. Front row: Alan Fisher, Tony Howells, Derek Mills. The teacher on the right is Mr Todd and the headmaster, Mr Lancaster, is on the left. During the time that Mr Lancaster was headmaster the school was involved in many activities both sporting and musical, all of which are recorded in a series of photograph albums still at the school. (Mrs Wheeler, Headteacher, All Saints School)

All Saints School open evening in 1953. The girls who are setting out the needlework display are, back: Anne Webley, Carol Plimmer, Sylvia Enefer; front: Joyce May and Sheila Brandreth. (Mrs Wheeler, Headteacher, All Saints School)

Class 1, St Stephen's School, with writing slates prominent on the desks and pupils displaying what appear to be items they have made. The sailor suits that several children are wearing would suggest this is a Victorian photograph as Queen Victoria promoted this fashion by dressing her children in similar suits. (Y5/STSTE/3)

Eastfield School choir in 1951. Among the children are Jean Griffiths, Pat Webb/Webster, Diana Woodwood, Maureen Harrison, Ann Webb/Webster, Christine Jones, Michael/Victor Jones, Michael Fry, Patrick McGhantry, John Franks, Grahame Holland, Eileen Jukes, Maureen and Jean Morby, Maureen Craft (now Hunt), Rita Bissell, Wendy Jarman, Maria Hickey, Winnie Hollywood, Maureen Rosier, Catherine/Cathleen Harrison, Valerie Smith, Glenis Beardson, Maria Jones, Joan Ingleby. (Maureen Hunt, Y5/EAST/1)

These two photographs are captioned Dudley Road Evening School. Several schools in the town held evening classes, often attended by young people who worked during the day. These two classes were actually held at the present Adult College in Old Hall Street around 1916. The young men appear to be studying science while the girls practise needlework in a very cramped space. The two photographs are romantically linked. The young man on the extreme left, centre, was Harold Edward Chambers, who worked during the day as a tool turner at Rees-Ro-Turbo and the girl marked with an 'X', fourth from the back, centre row, was Elsie Aldis. They met through the classes and married at St Paul's Church in September 1919. (John Chambers, I2/OLD/1&2)

Eight
Transport and Services

A hot air balloon ascent from the Molineux Grounds on Saturday 25 May 1901. The balloon was one of four Hudson's Soap war balloons which were facsimiles of those used by the military authorities in South Africa. It rose to a height of 1,000 ft by means of a cable attached to a traction engine and was filled with gas taken from pipes specially laid to the mains. Customers of Hudson's were given free tickets and the public were charged 10s for a ride. (T7/3)

The Birmingham Canal, with the Commercial Road power station in the background and a coal wharf in the foreground. (C. Johnson, Dave Rogers)

A more picturesque view of the Birmingham Canal at the Broad Street basin, taken around 1910. At this time there was still a considerable amount of traffic, with boats moored side by side. Note the horses, used for towing, enjoying some food. (Patrick Thorn, DB/BRO/8)

Opposite: Another view of the Birmingham Canal at a later date, showing the Mill Street bridge, part of J.N. Miller's flour mill and other industries that grew up near the waterway. The canal, engineered by James Brindley, was opened in stages from 1769 to 1772 and was used mainly to carry coal. (F. Nickholds, D7/BIR/2)

Wolverhampton High Level Station in June 1960, before modernisation began in 1964. The sign on the left directs passengers for the Low Level Station towards the passageway which connected the two. Wolverhampton acquired two stations very close together because of the

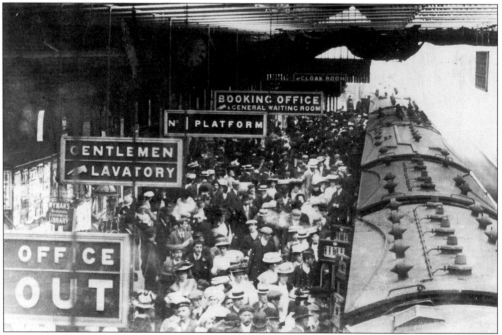

A crowded scene on No. 1 platform of the High Level station in 1908. It would appear to have been a public holiday owing to the number of passengers. Day trips were very popular at this time and had to be taken either by steam train or horse-drawn vehicle. The station officially lost its 'High Level' prefix in 1973. (Bennett Clark/Northicote School, K3/HIG/I/1)

bitter rivalry between the Great Western Railway and the London & North Western Railway. The High Level opened in 1852 and a first-class fare to Birmingham cost 2s 6d for a 40 minute journey. A second-class journey lasted 56 minutes and cost 1s 6d. (K3/HIG/E/6)

The Low Level Station, which opened in 1854. Trains ran from here to London on the Great Western line. The last booked train passed over the line at 00.43a.m. on Sunday 27 July 1969. The station became a parcels concentration depot in 1970 and finally closed on 4 October 1972. The future of the building is currently under debate, with plans for an exhibition and leisure-heritage centre under consideration. (J. Harper, K3/LOW/E/7)

The Midland Railway Excursion Office, which was part of the Victoria Hotel building in Lichfield Street when this photograph was taken in 1901. It included Cook's Excursion & Tourist Office and, in fact, Wolverhampton had one of Thomas Cook's earliest branches. Among the excursions on offer are cruises on the Orient Pacific line, a ten guinea tour of Rome and other Italian cities, or less exotic visits to the seaside or Worcester races. (L3/COOK/E/1)

A Lorain electric tram on its way to Newbridge, *c.* 1910. (S7/3)

Interested onlookers watch Wolverhampton's first trolleybus in Broad Street, October 1923. Trolleybuses were replaced by motor buses from the early 1960s and the last trolleybus in the town ran on 6 March 1967. (S5/4)

These experimental automatic traffic lights in Princes Square on 5 November 1927 were the first in the country. The installation was made by J. Boot, Chief Engineer for the Siemens & General Electric Railway Signal Co., and consisted of an aluminium signal box suspended above the centre of the road from cables with red, green and amber lights facing in four directions. This was only a one-day trial and a slightly different system was installed in October 1928. (P4/PRI/1)

The residence of the master of the Wolverhampton Union Workhouse, Bilston Road, c. 1900. The workhouse was opened in 1840 to house approximately 750 people, replacing the old workhouse in Horseley Fields which was built in 1700 and which subsequently became a temporary barracks. The Union Workhouse was unusual in being situated in the town centre as it was considered better for workhouses to be some distance away to ensure that only bona fide paupers made the journey. Chronic overcrowding led to the building of a new workhouse at New Cross to accommodate 1,242 inmates which opened on 24 September 1903. (J4/BIR/E/3)

The Workhouse Master, Mr E.J. Sattin, c. 1900. The Poor Law Amendment Act of 1834 allowed Poor Law Unions to appoint paid officials and Wolverhampton had, amongst others, a Medical Officer, Matron, and a rather unfortunately named Insane Attendant. The Master's salary in 1900 was £145. (J4/BIR/I/1)

The children's ward in the Union Workhouse, Bilston Road, in the late nineteenth century. Children seem to have made up about one third of workhouse inmates and severe overcrowding eventually resulted in the purchase of land at Wednesfield for the building of the Cottage Homes. These opened in 1890 and comprised four houses for boys and four for girls. When children reached the age of 13 they could be apprenticed out, usually into trades such as lock making and mining, although in 1887 half a dozen Wolverhampton children were apprenticed to the North Sea Steam Trawling Co. in Grimsby. (J4/BIR/I/7)

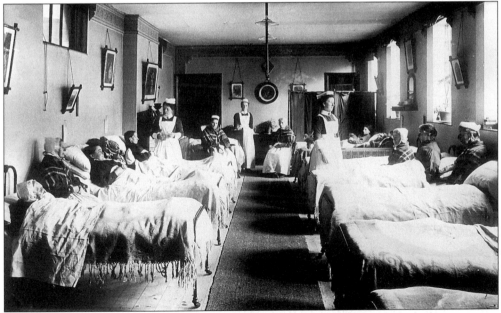

The women's ward in the Bilston Road workhouse, c. 1900. Every able-bodied woman was expected to do the domestic work of the house: scrubbing, cleaning, knitting and sewing. In addition, they also had to pick oakum, which involved untwisting old rope to obtain loose fibre, used for caulking ships' seams, stopping up leaks and sometimes for dressing wounds. (J4/BIR/I/8)

The Wolverhampton Gas Co. building on the corner of Darlington Street and Waterloo Road. Built in 1880, it was replaced in 1939 with a new showroom which still stands today. (H6/WOL/E/1)

The new gas showrooms on the same site pictured on 2 January 1940, a short time before opening. Signs in the windows direct customers to a temporary showroom in Waterloo Road. The building is now occupied by a travel agency and mobile phone retail store after a number of years as home to Sun Alliance & London Insurance and Allied Carpets. (H6/WOL/E/12)

Wolverhampton Corporation
Electrical Department, Red Lion
Street, *c.* 1930, advertising toasters
at 23s 6d, electric kettles at 67s
6d, and electric tea urns at 75s.
Other items for sale include
vacuum cleaners, pedestal fires,
milk heaters, immersion heaters
and table breakfast cookers.
(H8/ELEC/I/2)

Commercial Road Power Station,
built in 1894. It started to supply
Wolverhampton with electricity
in 1895. By 1929 an area of 100
square miles was served by
Wolverhampton Corporation
Electricity Department, which
included the town and
surrounding villages. The town
guide boasted that electricity
prices, at a flat rate of $4\frac{1}{2}$d, were
'amongst the lowest in the
country'. (H9/MUN/E/1)

The Wolverhampton and South Staffordshire General Hospital, Cleveland Road, erected during 1846-8 on land purchased from the Duke of Cleveland and opened on 1 January 1849. It was designed by Edward Banks to house 100 beds. In 1937 the General Hospital was part of a group of hospitals, known as the Royal Hospital, which also included the Bath Road Maternity Home, The Beeches, The Sister Dora Convalescent Home at Milford, and the Women's Hospital. The only one to survive is the General, which is now known as the Royal Hospital, and this is due to close in March 1997, although the building will be preserved. (J1/ROY/E/1)

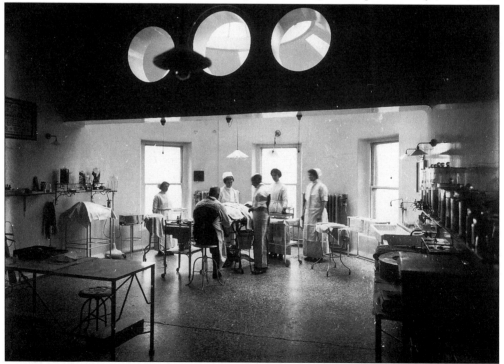

The General Hospital operating theatre, which was officially opened on 24 July 1896. (J1/ROY/I/1)

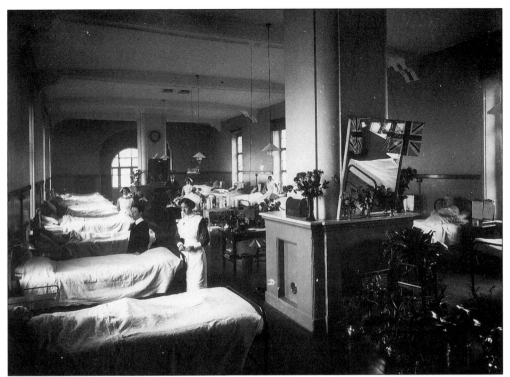

Ward 9 (the boys' ward) at the Royal Hospital, *c.* 1910 (J1/ROY/I/2, J1/ROY/I/7)

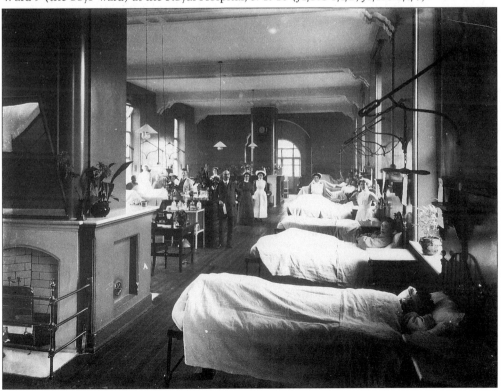

A garden party at the Eye Infirmary, possibly the one organised in 1909 by Joseph Jones, Chairman of the Board. The original eye infirmary opened in 1881 in a rented house in St Mark's Place, Chapel Ash. The present building was opened on 23 October 1888. Philip Horsman donated £5,000, which covered the cost of building the in-patient department. (J1/EYE/E/2)

Wolverhampton & District Hospital for Women, Park Road West, photographed from West Park. A dispensary for women was opened in 1886 in Cleveland Road and moved into the building vacated by the Eye Infirmary in 1890. The building pictured was opened in 1904 with 24 in-patient beds in eight wards. It was extended several times, including in 1928 when it amalgamated with the Royal Hospital. Many of the town's babies were born there before the gynaecological department was moved to New Cross in 1975. The hospital was re-named West Park Hospital and this building was demolished in 1978. (J1/WOM/E/2)